Shakespearean Swear Words Coloring Book

CONTAINS ADULT LANGUAGE AND IS NOT SUITABLE FOR CHILDREN

Villain, I have done thy mother

The rankest
compound of
villainous
smell

Thou
abortive,
rooting
hog!

Away, you bull's pizzle, you stock-fish!

Thou art a boil, a plague sore.

Would thou wert clean enough to spit upon

Would thou wouldst burst!

Poisonous
bunch-backed
toad!

Away, you three-inch fool!

I scorn you,
scurvy
companion!

I'll beat thee, but I would infect my hands

I am sick
when I do
look on thee

Methink'st
thou art a
general
offence!

You poor, rascally, cheating lack-linen mate!

Peace, ye fat guts!

Thou lump
of foul
deformity!

Thou whoreson zed, thou unnecessary letter!

Thou art
unfit for
any place
but hell.

Thy tongue outvenoms all the worms of Nile!

Thou damned and luxurious mountain goat!

Manufactured by Amazon.ca
Acheson, AB

15897363R00024